Grade 8 Piano
Sight Reading Intensive Exercise

(Based on ABRSM Grade 8
Piano Sight Reading Syllabus)

Regina Pratley

ISBN: 153061841X
ISBN-13: 978-1530618415

DEDICATION

Dedicated to all the students that are going to take the ABRSM grade 8 piano exam.
Wishing you all the best in the exam! ☺

CONTENTS

Tips for a Good Performance in Sight Reading

Be careful with the following things:

1. **Accidentals**
   Accidentals (Sharps/ Flats/ Naturals) on the previous notes in the same bar.

2. **Easily mistaken notes:**
   D#, E#, A#, B#
   C^b, F^b, G^b

3. **Peal Markings**
   a) Press and release the sustained (right) pedal:

   P_____⌋

   b) Likewise for the rest of the bars:
   simile
   P_____⌋

   c) *con ped*= Use the sustained (right) pedal for the whole piece, you have to determine yourself when to press and release the pedal:

   d) *una corda*= press the left pedal
   e) *tre corde*= release the left pedal

4. **Octave markings:**
   a) An octave higher:
   8va⌐⁻⁻⁻⁻⁻⁻⌐ or just "8va"/ "8" over a note

   b) An octave lower
   8vb--------⌋ or just "8vb"/ "8va" / "8" under a note

5. **Clef change**

6. **Articulations**
   staccato/ legato/ accents…

7. **Tempo**

8. **Dynamics**

A Fresh Breeze

A Relaxing Afternoon

Living in the Dream

Karma

Goodbye

Moderato

Requiem

Tragedy

A Starry Night

In the Park

Happiness

Sunshine

Unforgettable Love

The Hidden Pain

A Beautiful Day

The Moon Behind the Clouds

Ballade

A Thanksgiving Prayer

Sadness

Andante mesto

For the Sake of Your Dream

A Misty Dream

From Day to Night

A Sorrowful Night

Childhood

Memories

Dusk

A Better Tomorrow

You're the Winner!

Fate

Happy Dance

The Shadow

In the Church

Holiday

Folk Dance

The Pale Moon

Moderato mesto

A Sad Ending

Love for You

Lost and Found

The Best is Yet to Come

Printed in Great Britain
by Amazon

CAMERON MACKINTOSH
PRESENTS

IAN McSHANE

LUCIE
ARNAZ

MARIA
FRIEDMAN

JOANNA
RIDING

THE WITCHES OF EASTWICK

WITH

ROSEMARY
ASHE

PETER
JÖBACK

CAROLINE
SHEEN

STEPHEN
TATE

IN

A MUSICAL COMEDY

BOOK & LYRICS BY
JOHN DEMPSEY

BASED ON THE NOVEL BY
JOHN UPDIKE
AND
THE WARNER BROS.
MOTION PICTURE

MUSIC BY
DANA P ROWE

MUSICAL SUPERVISION
DAVID CADDICK

MUSICAL DIRECTOR
DAVID WHITE

ORCHESTRATIONS
WILLIAM DAVID BROHN

DANCE ARRANGEMENTS
DANA P ROWE & CHRISTOPHER JAHNKE

SOUND DESIGN
ANDREW BRUCE

LIGHTING DESIGN
HOWARD HARRISON

PRODUCTION DESIGN
BOB CROWLEY

CHOREOGRAPHY
BOB AVIAN & STEPHEN MEAR

DIRECTION
ERIC SCHAEFFER

WORLD PREMIERE AT THE THEATRE ROYAL DRURY LANE, TUESDAY 18TH JULY 2000

THE WitCHES OF EAStWICK

"DEVILISHLY GOOD FUN"

MICHAEL BILLINGTON **THE GUARDIAN**

VOCAL SELECTIONS FROM

THE WITCHES OF EASTWICK

Note: In the latest impression of this matching folio, the prelims have been shortened by four pages to remove out-of-date information. Printed page 12 is therefore actual page 8 in this edition.

© International Music Publications Ltd
First published in 2000 by International Music Publications Ltd
International Music Publications Ltd is a Faber Music company
3 Queen Square, London WC1N 3AU
Songbook arranged and edited by Stephen Metcalfe
Production photographs: Michael Le Poer Trench
Additional photographs: Alessandro Pinna
TM © CML designed by Dewynters plc London
Printed in England by Caligraving Ltd
All rights reserved

ISBN10: 0-571-52997-6   EAN13: 978-0-571-52997-1

To buy Faber Music publications or to find out about the full range of titles available,
please contact your local music retailer or Faber Music sales enquiries:

Faber Music Ltd, Burnt Mill, Elizabeth Way, Harlow, CM20 2HX England
Tel: +44(0)1279 82 89 82   Fax: +44(0)1279 82 89 83
sales@fabermusic.com   fabermusic.com

ACT ONE:

In the small New England town of Eastwick, Rhode Island, live three unhappy divorcees (our not-so-wicked witches)-- Alexandra Spofford, Jane Smart and Sukie Rougemont -- much to the chagrin of the town's self-appointed first citizen, Felicia Gabriel.

Failed sculptress Alexandra is concerned with her teenaged son, Michael, and his romance with Felicia's college-bound daughter, Jennifer. Uptight music teacher Jane is grappling with her divorce from her purportedly gay husband. And Sukie is troubled over her tedious affair with Clyde, Felicia's husband and editor of the paper where Sukie works.

One stormy night, over a heady brew of brownies and weak martinis, they wish for their perfect man **(MAKE HIM MINE)**.

In no time at all, the town's legendary Lenox House is bought, and its grounds ecologically disfigured, by a stranger from New York City -- one Darryl Van Horne. Sweeping into town atop a wave of gossip, the charismatic newcomer makes a sardonic case for small town living.

One night, not long after, Van Horne whisks Alexandra away to his oceanside manse, romancing, repulsing, and chiding her for failing to see the beauty in herself.

As Jane practices her cello the next evening, Darryl comes to call, violin in hand. Playing a duet with her, he unleashes the passion both in her music and her soul **(WAITING FOR THE MUSIC TO BEGIN)**.

Two down. One left.

The following day, Van Horne intrudes upon Sukie's home, questioning her seeming inability to finish a sentence. He remedies the problem **(WORDS, WORDS, WORDS)**.

If the three women are initially jealous when they discover that Darryl has been dividing his attentions between them, magic and sensuality soon win the day. And the night.

Back in town, Jennifer and Michael are dreading Jennifer's impending departure for Berkeley to attend college. They pledge their love for one another, doing their not-too-impressive best to name what it is they share **(SOMETHING)**.

Meanwhile, Eastwick is awash with rumors of Van Horne and his veritable harem. Felicia seizes the opportunity to rally her troops and get her daughter safely away from this carnal insanity **(DIRTY LAUNDRY)**.

On their way to the Lenox House, the three women reflect upon both their childhood dreams and their recent transformations. Darryl, watching them, marvels at his handiwork. Once arrived, they use a charmed cookie jar, cursing Felicia with a variety of objects -- tennis balls, bracelets, feathers -- which come flying out of her mouth. Enraptured and enamored, the three witches are sent sailing into the New England skies **(I WISH I MAY)**.

ACT TWO:

Months have passed. And if Felicia and her cronies have only grown more single-minded in their pursuits, so has Alexandra **(ANOTHER NIGHT AT DARRYL'S)**.

Darryl wanders into the middle of Michael's shift at Nemo's Diner, where he conjures up a preternatural lesson in the ways of the fairer sex for the lovelorn boy and the men of Eastwick **(DANCE WITH THE DEVIL)**.

The ladies and Darryl continue to plague Felicia, pouring thumb tacks, toenail clippings, spiders and cherry pits into the magic cookie jar…and out of Felicia's vile mouth.

In her kitchen, Felicia is stricken by the spell, even as she attempts to harangue her husband. Clyde ends it all with a well-timed frying pan, only to be extinguished himself in Felicia's dying breath **(EVIL)**.

News of Clyde and Felicia's mysterious deaths swiftly spreads through the town. Jennifer comes home from college to clear out the house. A newly educated Michael is chasing after every girl in Eastwick. Alexandra, Jane and Sukie, filled with guilt, distance themselves from Darryl. And an abandoned Darryl is none to happy about it, vowing revenge upon his distaff coven.

Coming across Jennifer at the docks, a remorseful Sukie ruminates on the ever-present past **(LOOSE ENDS)**.

Van Horne moves in on the orphan girl, however, and under his considerable influence, Jennifer is seduced. The two quickly become engaged to be married -- a fact rubbed squarely in the pretty faces of Alexandra, Jane and Sukie.

The women make their plans, even as Van Horne prepares for his wedding, gloating all the while **(WHO'S THE MAN?)**.

On the blessed day, Alexandra, Jane and Sukie crash the proceedings at the church. Armed with a wax effigy and a hat pin, they cast Darryl out of Eastwick.

Alexandra, Jane and Sukie have all found peace with themselves and their lives, poised to live happily ever after **(LOOK AT ME)**. Darryl Van Horne is out of their lives forever.

Perhaps…

"A SCINTILLATING AND THEATRICAL MUSICAL SHOW"
NICHOLAS DE JONGH **LONDON EVENING STANDARD**

"**MUSICAL COMEDY HEAVEN**"

GEORGINA BROWN **MAIL ON SUNDAY**

"A WICKEDLY ENJOYABLE SHOW
CASTS ITS SPELL ON LONDON"

JAMES INVERNE **TIME MAGAZINE**

"IT SENDS YOU OUT INTO THE NIGHT
WITH A SPRING IN YOUR STEP
AND A SMILE ON YOUR FACE"

CHARLES SPENCER **DAILY TELEGRAPH**

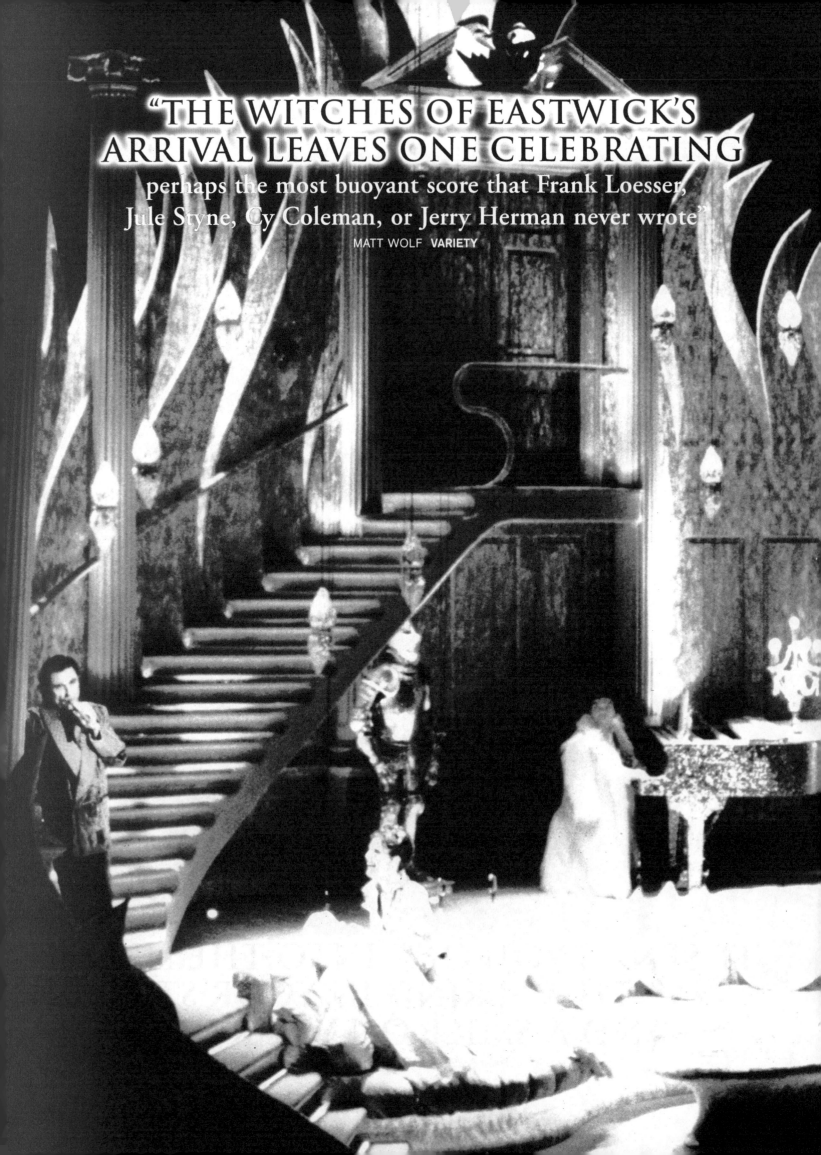

"THE WITCHES OF EASTWICK'S ARRIVAL LEAVES ONE CELEBRATING

perhaps the most buoyant score that Frank Loesser, Jule Styne, Cy Coleman, or Jerry Herman never wrote"

MATT WOLF **VARIETY**

Make Him Mine

WORDS BY JOHN DEMPSEY
MUSIC BY DANA P ROWE

14

Waiting For The Music To Begin

Words by John Dempsey
Music by Dana P Rowe

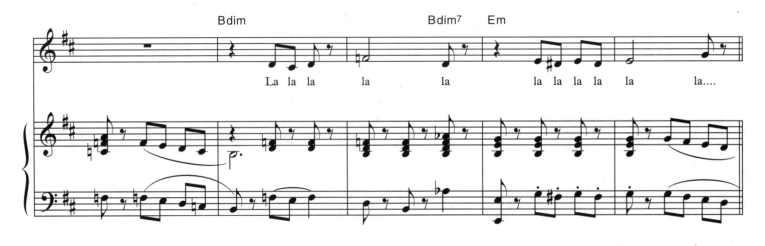

La la la la la la la la la la la....

So I grew up, pol-ished and prac - ticed.

Words, Words, Words

Words by John Dempsey
Music by Dana P Rowe

42

Something

Words by John Dempsey
Music by Dana P Rowe

Dirty Laundry

Words by John Dempsey
Music by Dana P Rowe

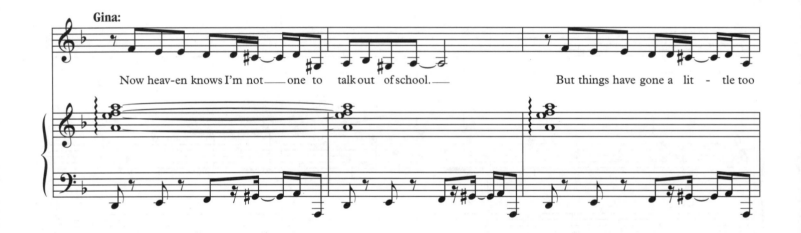

Now heav-en knows I'm not — one to talk out of school. — But things have gone a lit - tle too

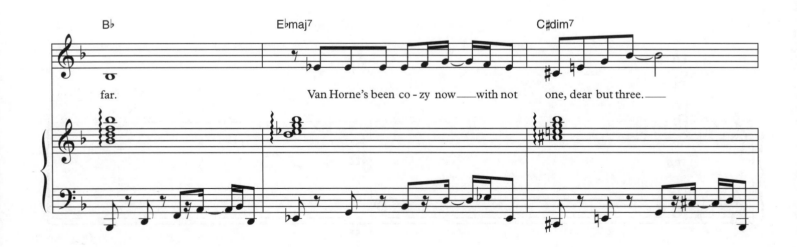

far. Van Horne's been co - zy now — with not one, dear but three. —

I Wish I May

Words by John Dempsey
Music by Dana P Rowe

Two per-fect cars. She asked the moon. She wished on stars.

Sukie: Once u-pon a time, a lit-tle girl, used to laze a-bout the lake, used to

Once u-pon a time, that girl was me...

swim in it at dawn, with all her clos-est girl-friends, not a stitch of cloth-ing on. They im-

-a-gined when a-lone how they might change when they were grown. Yet when the stars

66

Another Night At Darryl's

Words by John Dempsey
Music by Dana P Rowe

Dance With The Devil

Words by John Dempsey
Music by Dana P Rowe

Evil

Words by John Dempsey
Music by Dana P Rowe

Loose Ends

Words by John Dempsey
Music by Dana P Rowe

Who's The Man?

Words by John Dempsey
Music by Dana P Rowe

Look At Me

Words by John Dempsey
Music by Dana P Rowe

COME DANCE WITH THE DEVIL

How do these things start? We get asked that a lot. Words? Music? Neither, really. In the musical theatre, it starts with a story.

And that's where we found ourselves two years ago. In search of a subject. A title. A few words on a piece of paper. Simple enough? It's the stuff of nightmares!

Well… our nightmares, anyway.

After grinding our wheels and teeth for some time, Cameron Mackintosh gave us a list from the Warner Brothers catalogue, listing properties they thought might be prime candidates for musicalisation. Dozens of great titles. But as we made our way through the alphabetised list, it became dishearteningly clear there wasn't much there that 'sang.' For ultimately, what makes a movie great is full use of the medium of film itself – be it the intimacy of the close-up or the grandeur of sweeping vistas. Finding a movie with a structure broad enough, characters large enough, passions oversized enough to meet the needs of the musical stage was going to be difficult. Factor in personal taste, and our desire to do something both comedic and magical, and the task looked outright impossible.

But there, on the very last page of that list, nestled snugly in the Ws was THE WITCHES OF EASTWICK. This had possibilities. A contemporary sense of humour, a clear theme of self-empowerment, an intriguing (and theatrically well-tested) small town setting, and in Darryl Van Horne an extraordinary character for the male lead.

Most importantly, we had the chance to write three female characters that were women in the truest sense. Alexandra Spofford, Jane Smart and Sukie Rougemont. Neither villains nor victims, virgins nor whores, these three women were complete, complex and human in ways that women generally aren't in musicals these days. And yet, they would work fully as musical theatre creations. Individually, they were artistic, needful souls. Collectively, they could be a powerhouse. We swore then and there to write them in warm, womanly tones, abandoning the vocal gymnastics that are the trend these days.

Our initial batch of songs included two for our leading man, one operatic and deadly serious (called 'Fires of Creation,' no less), the other being "Who's the Man?" One worked. One did not. And so it went. The form and tone were finding their way. Much to our surprise, we found ourselves writing a proper book musical. And more than that – a proper American musical comedy.

The first year of this process was bliss. We'd work six days a week, fuelled by good source material (God bless John Updike), and strong coffee (God bless Starbucks). Every few months, Cameron (God bless him, while we're at it) would come to New York and we would perform a little cabaret act for him of what we had written.
Of the first batch of six songs, five survived.
Of the next batch of six songs, five also survived.
The fate of the next batch of six songs is better left unspoken. Bit by bit by bit the score and the book fell into place.

The next year saw our little three-person clubhouse expanding rapidly. Eric Schaeffer joined the team. Then Bob Crowley, Howard Harrison and Andrew Bruce; David Caddick, David White and Bill Brohn; Bob Avian and Stephen Mear. Inestimable talents, all. When the show was cast, thirty-five more souls were added to the collective. Assistants were brought in. Advertising people, copyists, marketing strategists, production managers, musicians, publicists, stage managers. The first day of rehearsal alone had a larger audience than just about any show we'd done to date.

Yet for all that, it comes back to one decision, one small moment in time:

"We read the list, Cameron. What about THE WITCHES OF EASTWICK?"

"Yes, dear. That's the one I liked, too."

And that is how these things start.

John Dempsey and Dana P Rowe
June, 2000

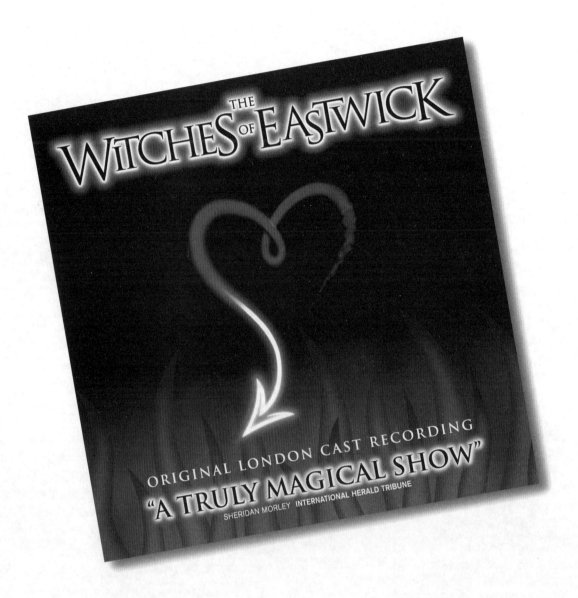